"Night has its owl, day its hawk / and every remembering is a forgetting." Wit~~h~~ bird life and huus sparrow soar Through clear st understand and poems, we hear the birds' voices telling us what to listen for. Each poem in *The Double Nest* is an adventure of flying out, getting lost, and coming home. These are poems to revisit often!

—Maureen Buchanan Jones
author of *Maude and Addie*
and *blessed are the menial chores*

In *The Double Nest*, a book of mostly poems in couplet form, Rhett Watts writes the old and new worlds in synch with earth's quotidian rhythms: dawn, day, dusk, and dark. The poems double as visual and aural, sometimes even swap places, hearing what is seen, like birdsong, beginning with the aubade, "Bird Hours." "The Double Nest" is also a title poem on the poet's brother's death. How does she handle the dark? in the ways we all do, with humor and imagination. In "Cat and Mouse": "Will I hear my rendezvous approach / Like the tick tock of Captain Hook's croc, / Or will it arrive torpedo...deep, silent, fast?" Highly recommended!

—Donna Fleischer
author of *Baby in Space*
and *F L A N E U R*

Rhett Watts' *The Double Nest*, is an ever-deepening meditation on a dazzling array of subjects, on self and the cosmos ("These days I see my body as a planet"), on the inscrutability of nature, on mourning a beloved, on memory, art, and history. What a joy it is, slipping into a poetic sensibility embedded in nature able to give the double experience of precise descriptions of creatures with the immediate subjective responses of the poet.

Watts interweaves the two together: "The photograph writes with light / Shutter quick a wings." If you are looking for a poetic vision that shows the marks of a hard-won wisdom and mature spiritual being, this book is for you.

—Marilyn E. Johnston
author of *Weight of the Angel*
and *Downward Dreaming*

Like the song of the wood thrush that emanates from the dapple light of wooded glades, Watts conveys to us that which by emotion cannot be expressed in ordinary spoken language; wherever you are, wherever you have been, and no matter who you are, you will realize that your journey was not quite so alone. This collection brings nature and poetry together; birds are the backdrops for experiences, moods, times, and places. Her words connect us.

—Robert Tougias
author of *Birder on Berry Lane*
and *Quest for the Eastern Cougar*

Cohorts of birds and mammals cohabit this remarkable and satisfying collection. Pages teem with animal sights and sounds foundational to the poems' meanings. When a "Cormorant spreads wings like a priest's arms," an elegy unfolds. A clockface by M.C. Escher featuring "a chime of wrens winging" hangs majestically in a poem's mosaic of memories. *The Double Nest* celebrates the slow work of building a personal relationship with nature. Memories of youthful daring become cautionary tales when advancing years have you "swimming with the crocodiles now." Solace can come with being "Alone, not lonesome..." Watts beckons us to her side where we, too, can be lovestruck by beauty.

—Judith Ferrara
author of *A Feast of Losses: Yetta Dine*
and Her Son, the Poet Stanley Kunitz

The Double Nest

Rhett Watts

Fernwood
PRESS

The Double Nest
©2025 by Rhett Watts

Fernwood Press
Newberg, Oregon
www.fernwoodpress.com

All rights reserved. No part may be reproduced
for any commercial purpose by any method without
permission in writing from the copyright holder.

Printed in the United States of America

Cover and page design: Eric Muhr
Cover photo: Rhett Watts
Author photo: Elizabeth Pope

ISBN 978-1-59498-172-2

*In memory of my brother Steve
and
for Bob who loves birds*

Contents

Acknowledgments 11
Bird Hours 14
DAWN 15
The Doorway Effect 16
Sub-Versive 17
House Holds 18
Shadows 19
Cold Snap 20
Poemania 21
Pedal Pushers 22
Approaching Equinox 24
Bonfire (2021) 25
Floating Arms 26
Forced Spring 27
Available Music 28
Rose-breasted Grosbeak 29
The Little Hours 30
Entranced 31

Ask the Animals 32
At Slack Tide 33

DAY 35
Brookside 36
Bear and Wolf 37
On De-extinction 38
When Wood Dies 39
After the Gold Rush 40
Beast with No Name 42
Lament 43
Almost Paradise 44
Book of the Dead 46
Bird Fish 48
The Double Nest 49
Visitation 50
Rhythm Changes 51
Invasives 52
Lughnasadh / Lammas 53
Learning One Good Place 54

DUSK 55
Ode to My Belly 56
Furculas 58
Celestial Bodies 59
The Mending 60
Remembering the Frog State 61
The Flying Monk—1055 A.D. 62
Contacting My Muse 64
Jerome's Lion 66
Coming to Terms 67
The Rental 68
Wisdom Is a Bird 70
Dark Brook 71
Nest Fidelity in Two Movements 72

Homing 74
DARK 75
Desire Path 76
Grounded.. 77
One Day, May 25, 2020 78
Darwin's Tree and Escher's Birds 79
The Problem..80
The Symbiocene: wished-for time of deeper integration
    between humans and all the natural world 81
Blues for Betty 82
Cat and Mouse 84
Bond of Union, lithograph, M.C. Escher 85
Signs and Wonders..86
Slow Work 87
Pieced Out 88
Orison for the Wee Hours 89

Notes 91
Title Index 93
First Line Index 97

Acknowledgments

Grateful acknowledgment is made to the editors of the following publications in which these poems first appeared, some in earlier versions:

Amethyst Review: "The Little Hours," "Slow Work"
Canary: A Literary Journal of the Environmental Crisis: "The Mending," "Bear and Wolf"
Glacial Hills Review: "Grounded," "Entranced"
Moonstone Arts Center: One Hundred Thousand Poets for Change: "One Day (May 25, 2020)"
One Art Journal: "Coming to Terms"
Passager Journal: "At Slack Tide"
Persimmon Tree: "The Doorway Effect"
PoetryMagazine.com: "Ode to my Belly"
Presence: An International Journal of Spiritual Companionship: "Bird Hours"
Relief: A Journal of Art and Faith: "Floating Arms"
San Pedro River Review: "Homing"
Soul-Lit: A Journal of Spiritual Poetry: "Jerome's Lion"
The Christian Century: "On De-Extinction"
The Kerf: "Remembering the Frog State," "Learning One Good Place"

The Orchards Poetry Journal: "The Double Nest"
The Raven's Perch: "Sub-Versive," "Beast with No Name"
The Windhover: "The Flying Monk"
The Worcester Review: "Blues for Betty," "After the Gold Rush"
Vita Poetica Journal: "Ask the Animals"

*But ask the animals what they think—let them teach you;
let the birds tell you what's going on.
Put your ear to the earth—learn the basics.*
             *—*from Job, *The Message*

Bird Hours

Ribbon of first light
welcome long-awaited one
chanted here by song.

*

Mockingbird morning.
Red ladybugs everywhere—
busy little hours.

*

Yellow-rumped warblers
dip and glide along the brook.
Happiness ripples.

*

Pinnacle of morn—
afternoon's Ready, set—
robin gets her worm.

*

Now shadows lengthen.
Finish tasks with gracefulness.
Smooth ruffled feathers.

*

A bevy of quail
enter into in-between.
Rest, a kind of work.

*

Sounds heard in the dark—
a constellation of starlings
bathing in night.

Dawn

The Doorway Effect

Eyes open to the uncommon
beauty of common grackles beyond

my window. They chortle and crake—
Quisculas quiscala.

I stumble out of bed like an old-timer
in an old movie. First face-splash,

a thank offering for another day.
Last night's dream scenes dissolve

in a camera cutaway as I walk back
into the bedroom.

What did I come in here for?

I read that passing under a doorway
resets memory, prompts a new episode.

Get up to pee and dream lines leak
out your ear onto the pillow.

Night has its owl, day its hawk
and every remembering is a forgetting.

In sleep, eyes dart back and forth—
an actor scanning a script.

Before the prompter cues,
before coffee, I would glide awhile

a bird woman slipping like smoke,
like water around the edges.

Sub-Versive

A gang of street urchins
fills balloons with flame from a tank
used to inflate silks of hot-air balloons.

The Keystone cop walks his beat,
swinging his billy club. Whistling, he looks
the other way, seems not to notice

ragamuffins forming a human chain.
They pass bags that burn but are not ruined.
Hand to hand, the fire balloons sink

into the gutter, then deeper down a manhole.
Waking, I am glad to catch the mudlarks
at work. As long as they stoke my belly

and the mind patrol that has dogged me
for weeks is distracted, I can write.

House Holds

Housewarming to mortgage burning,
our dwellings cradle, charm, chastise us.

The top stair creaks, marking the start
and finish of each day.

Brass door-knocker sounds arrivals
and interruptions. Furnace sighs

in the basement, both annoying
and taking the chill off.

Gurgling potted fern delights
and guilts me when finally watered.

A swift in the chimney,
raindrops pinging in the flue.

O my beloved vexations.

Silent slide of honey off a spoon
slow as dust motes in sunbeams.

Garlic brightens taste buds
and sours my breath.

Wood musk stays cornered in
the fireplace though the fire is out.

Last year's leaves stain the cement walk
after the gold is swept away

and the unmade bed keeps my husband's
shape even after he's gone.

Shadows

They also occupy rooms—
yours, mine. Key found under

the potted plant by the screen door;
they enter and remain.

Glimpsed behind barred windows,
quick as a flickering eyelid.

Not the known guests welcomed,
those who blow life into you.

Hidden co-travelers, friendly and
otherwise, caravan inside us

like genetic code. Some social
as café chatter or purring pigeons

gathered on a roof. Others are
known only by what is left behind:

a misplaced magazine, backdoor ajar,
the stale smell of cigarettes or

a tendency toward depression.
And I wonder when trespassers

become homesteaders squatting
in the space once called the soul.

Cold Snap

Before the storm, before I shoot,
mist rises off the creek in our backyard,
ice dams crackling.

      Chickadees swoop limb to limb
like socks wheeled out on clothesline
hung slack between the hemlocks.

The temperature drops,
ice crystals grow a skin, link
the stream banks. My body chills,

lens focuses, sensor gathers rays.
The photograph writes with light.
Shutter quick as wings.

Poemania

All nature speaks, and ev'n ideal things
flap shadowy sounds from visionary wings.
         —E. A. Poe

Sometimes memories pile in a wreck of years.
Other times, they come like falling into
a stack of laundry, still warm.

We poets, circle like hawks—
Nature, Love, Time or Mortality,
time as it relates to creatures.

Poemania is not a slick hair gel
once made of bear fat.
That's pomade. And it's not

a province in Northern Poland
or a breed of fluffy dogs.
Pomerania and Pomeranian.

Not the inventor of the detective story,
Edgar Allan Poe. It is a literary compulsion,
the affliction of writing poems.

Pedal Pushers

The bike hangs on our shed wall,
sidelined for the season.

Frozen spikes recall the cold cloud hung
over the world in a veil of volcanic ash

during our last "Little Ice Age" after the
volcanic eruption of 1816, year without

a summer. Dimmed sun, dry fog, and
red snow fired up Turner's sunsets in oil.

Birthed Mary Shelly's monster penned
by candlelight during a dark noon.

Crops failed, people and animals starved
as monsoons shifted, rivers overflowed.

Prompted by the shortage of horses,
a German aristocrat built the first bicycle.

The Dandy Horse, clunky contraption
of wood and metal fitted with brakes,

no pedals. Iron-wheeled bone-shaker,
it altered even the history of underclothes.

Corsets and bustles gave way to bloomers
and by our time, cropped pants.

I raced my first bike, a blue Rambler,
downhill and up. My freedom machine.

The beauty of the bicycle: human-propelled
yet reliant on the goodwill of

wealthy innovators. Weird weather
and temperature swings set me wondering

about the wheels we have set spinning—
all pedals, no brakes.

Approaching Equinox

Icy branches glisten.
Droplets fall in a second rain
slow as unnamed griefs.

Winds sweep clouded woods.
Sudden sun, and water crystals flash—
ruby citron cobalt.

Out of sync with my seasons,
weathers, I would stay winter,
its still snows deepening.

Bonfire (2021)

from the Middle English "bone fyre"

Snow in patches.
A day moon between pitch pines.

Gibbous, waning only to the eye,
a whole note partially erased

and scored on a disappeared line.
It is hard to hear the moon's music.

I open my window to the scent of pine
as wind sets branches droning.

Stare into the photo our son sent
of Boston folk bundled by an open fire.

Unmasked, they sit semi-circle
on benches of packed snow

filling a few parking spaces.
Boombox blaring,

wood smoke mingles with breath.
Lulled, their hooded shadows rest

into night. Lean into remembrance,
celebrate survival.

Our son stopped there on his way home
to warm his hands awhile.

Floating Arms

The eve before the Irish first day of spring,
Brighid walks the land.

Sun on oak floors, I push the mop to the scent
of Murphy's oil soap,

feeling fierce as the warrior queen I was
this morning arguing with my mate.

Central heat against the biting blue and
the Danish word for coziness slips my mind.

Wipe the counter, put the kettle on. Ache spreads
over me like robins landing in the juniper.

Protectress of children, midwives, Brighid shapeshifts
into birds. And I miss the solace of a mother.

Would offer mine a cuppa, but like the robins,
she is on the other side of glass.

Women lay cloths or ribbons for the saint, the goddess
to bless as she passes between seasons.

Beneath your mantle, keep us from harm,
from ignorance, from heartlessness.

Neither winter nor spring, Brighid's mother gave birth
to her straddling the threshold of a dairy.

      Standing in my doorframe, I press the backs
of wrists hard into the jams as I did when a kid.

Hold, then drop them stepping out of the frame,
arms slowly rise as if catching air.

Forced Spring

Bulb of the buried flower
needs cooling to send green thumbs
from lobes papered like cloves of garlic.

Paperwhites, amaryllis strain
like the voices of young sopranos
who peak before their time.

Squirrel delicacies, some emerge
from bent stems. Others put off
blossoming to multiply in the dirt.

Spring surprises with a set of
butterfly wings in the juniper.
A bee curled on a leaf.

Not dead, asleep. A male banished
from the hive or female out all night.
She may be next year's queen.

Available Music

From what direction does it come?
All directions in rustled feather,
the warbling throats of yardbirds.

Raucous sparrow orgy
in the hemlocks. Branches swishing
like brushes on a snare drum.

The clack and rattle of a jay
are backdrop to a live set swinging
to percussive twigs snapped by

an unseen neighbor. Listen
for gusts that blow the heads off
dandelions gone to seed.

Each bird announces clear as the
clatter of wind chimes belling,
punctuated by the beagle's bark,

the clang of trash cans trucked
through the neighborhood.
Enter a finch crafting a fretwork of

found twine and weeds to the tempo
of the everyday. Here, where trills
and bangs are heard as song.

Even the close refrain of a wasp
trying at knots in a post,
looking for a way into wood.

Rose-breasted Grosbeak

Before I sight him, the shy bird
sounds robin-like, sweeter.

Crimson chevron on white breast,
black and white wings flashing.

The patch is clot-like, swollen
as if to seal a leaky vessel.

Family ruptures are said to heal
through his genial song.

Foliage gleaner, cousin to the cardinal,
Cut-throat is his poor nickname.

Call him instead, Balm for the bruised,
and Mender of broken spirit bones.

His brown-streaked mate sports a white
line over each eye as they sing

to each other nesting. Spell
one another to feed. Favor the edge

of thicket and stream, tall trees.
Other birds flown, grosbeak lands

at the feeder for black oil seed.
Returned weaver of nests,

of melody, like the dawn
first a song and I listen.

The Little Hours

Mid-morn, noon, mid-afternoon,
paired doves dab for seed

where the lawn meets asphalt and
the courting male calls.

Mottled feathers, blue-ringed eyes,
mourning doves hunt and peck

during the hours formerly known as
terce, sext, none.

Without the drama of dawn or dusk,
time for stacked paperwork,

cups of tea. Value measured by
ticked to-do lists. Dollar-time.

The twice-twelved day sliced fine
needs thicker layers, a kinder pace.

Praise for eyes that stare off,
soften focus. For deep sighs

body releases from our first dwelling
in the world. Thanks also

for the doves who wing whistle
and like the hours, flee.

Entranced

Draped in sheers, my cat contemplates
finches. An indoor kitty, once
I found him prone in grass,
a mockingbird sweeping over him.

Rivers of wind, dried leaves smack
against the house. Snake plant twists
beside me, the aloe holds her leaves
in a stilled wave.

The cat sleeps. I get up to turn
the music down.   Huge wings
fill the window a few feet from me.
Startled at the eagle's six-foot span,

pumping up from where bass hide
underwater, my neck cranes to watch
her circle. Crackling from the encounter,
I wonder if she saw me.

Feathers spread like fingertips,
muscled wings beating, sky ruler of day
and only glass between us.

Ask the Animals

Wolf spider on a flat rock splays
an inky star. What does the galloping brook
sound like to her?

Chipmunk clutches a wild rose stalk.
Arcing, swaying over the stream, he gages
the distance to the other bank.

Last spring, mating river snakes roiled and
scooted through the drought-dry streambed—
marvelous entanglement.

One night, I joined our housecat at the window.
Under the streetlamp, black bear ambled
to wherever it is she sleeps.

A home can be precarious. Given time,
given space, the heart may hold everything.
Maybe that is why we live so long.

Tiny hatchlings turtle through the grass.
Shells rough as the macadam they cross,
then plop into the creek. I lose count at fifty-three.

At Slack Tide

(the period of stillness just before the tide turns)

Now that I no longer take long walks,
he brings me things like the little green
pinecone he found in the woods.

It rests on my windowsill,
a placeholder for all that is
stunted and stunning.

He puts his jacket on and I say,
"Carry me with you, here,"
my hand on his breast pocket.

Smiling, he nods, then leaves.
Returns with tokens of the world:

a blue action figure fallen to the street

a nest blown from the eaves of a barn
he thinks he would like to own

a stone so smooth you could wear it
in your shoe.

Once, when I was feeling utterly low,
my eyes closed, he placed in my palm
a knobbed whelk shell.

Washed up
onto the local mud flats,
its salmon-colored insides opened me.

Day

Brookside

I call to myself today the musicality
of the cardinal, pluck of the jay,
and goldfinch's joie de vivre.

May thoughts rise as mist
from the brook's cool flow,
my body grounded as river stone.

Path clear as the way of bass
who know to both dart and glide.
And may I learn stability

of place like oak and ash.
Agility of the bounding cottontail.
And live in fellowship with luscious dirt,

ancient ferns, mosses, and all who
share birth, blood and breath.

Bear and Wolf

Finnish photographer documents unlikely pair

He shakes off den dreams, splashes
loping over brook stones—a bear on a ramble.
Dazzling, scent stronger than wet wool,
yelps echo like sliding rock.

Then up against a snag, his tongue reaches
for honeycomb as a wolf wigwags
at his feet. Back-scratching, the bear
seems not to notice.

She-wolf bows, dodging before
the standing bear who drops on all fours.
A single wolf is small threat. This night
and for nine nights more they roam,

companioned in the moonlit basin
until dawn. They even share prey throughout
their long truce. Parted, wolf enters the
shallows at dusk. Her pelt, the sky

both silver as the trout writhing
in her jaws. Bear probes for ants in the
cliff-face lined with veins of mica
lustrous in the setting sun.

On De-extinction

> *Scientists try to resurrect an extinct Australian frog by implanting cells in a related living species.*

She's rock-sitting in my mind's eye
beneath a riverine gallery of eucalyptus,
the platypus frog defunct. She swallows her
own glistening eggs. Strange stomach

that serves as womb. Clever the chemical
blocking acid that would digest her young as
so much caviar. She'll not eat again while
they grow inside. Belly bloated, lungs collapsed,

she breathes through moist skin.
Startled by researchers in rain, vomits up
six perfect froglets, guts turned out
like an emptied pocket. Ravaged by a fungus

running rampant in the amphibian world,
she's gone the way of Martha—last passenger pigeon.
May come back, Lady Lazarus of frogs,
the Gastric Brooder revived like the wished for

return of the Wooly Mammoth. And we,
selves within selves like stacking dolls.
What finely articulated if invisible beings
may be birthed out our silent mouths agape?

When Wood Dies

Windblown swamp maple—
seen from my second story

tree arborists call *hung-up*
leans on a nearby oak,

broken branch dangling.
Root ball half-exposed,

the maple falls forever
at 45 degrees. Free of the

cant hook, the felling blade
and nourished by sapwood,

heart rot's fruiting conks
spill out bark wounds.

I spot a woodpecker up
near the tilted crown,

hear him drill a cavity
for nesting.

That root-torn trunk may
yet become

mossy snug of fox,
lair of coiled rattler

waiting on the return
of the white-footed mouse.

After the Gold Rush

> *All in a dream, all in a dream the loading had begun*
> *Flying Mother Nature's silver seed to a new home in the sun.*
> —lyrics by Neil Young

Moonbeam, moon dream. Man-in-the-moon,
The Moon-Man, "Crazy Bob" Goddard, Worcester's own,
inventor of the liquid-fueled rocket.

1899, up a cherry tree, the watcher of bird flight, teenage
keeper of TNT in the attic, reader of H.G. Wells,
imagines a rocket blasting off in fields back of the barn.

Body knows first, thrust and drag in a wind-swayed tree,
sparking mind to screen a device that will travel
to Earth's satellite. Did he hold up a globed cherry to size

a day moon, pop it in his mouth, spit the pit earthward
falling like Newton's apple? Wonder how to escape the gravity
of his persistent illnesses? A childhood experiment:

to jump higher while scuffing a gravel walk like carpet
for a charge, battery in hand. It failed. Other attempts
quelled by Mother saying he might sail away.

Two decades after his vision, on Aunt Effie's farm,
now a golf course, the first of many launches ascends
forty-one feet off the ground.

1969, and Goddard's widow enthralled at the lift-off
of *Apollo 11*, "I don't know if I'm dreaming now,
or he was dreaming then."

Do the stars and stripes still wave on the moon?
Photos show only the flagpole's shadow. Moonstruck,
may our neighbor remain mythic partner, not merely

plundered source of rare minerals, water. Escape
of the rich. Waystation to Mars. May we dream well.
Moon shot, moon race. Moon rock, moon face.

Beast with No Name

Like a murmuration of starlings,
I rush a river. Sit on haunches like a cat
or potatoes in a field.

Favorite words are *dwell, bodacious,
beloved*. Hurts are shelved
like the bones of my kin.

I can forgive infidelities, my own,
others. And the ego that reigns supreme,
my own, others.

Would soar like the falcon, plunge
to ground in a skyfall. Mostly, glow with
wood's blue flame, hungry as the raptor.

I long to move with the presence of the bear.
Would be constant as the gray wolf. Yet,
am changeable as the phases of the moon.

Lament

Over a hundred birds fell out of the sky over Kansas.
Their wings may have been coated with ice.
           —from a radio news story

I would enter like a cow wandering in and out
doorways of a ruined manor. Follow the scent of water
like a turtle crossing the road.

Beached, waiting for the tide to shift, I search
pools for you, my moon snail, purple star fish.
Find only my wavering reflection.

You probably don't look like yourself anymore.
And I've lost the combination to your locker,
empty as the cages at Birdland. I would sing,

yet sound some off-key woodwind.
Would fly like the fallen birds of Kansas,
like a moth with wings of stone.

Almost Paradise

(1959)

I reach for Dad's hand as he rings the bell.
A man tall as he opens the white door.

Dad says he is the butler. They both smile.
Floorboards creaking, we are led down the hall.

Scent of cabbage boiling tells me its someone's
home. Not sure whose, folks bustling.

A mittened mascot, I accompany my father
on his old-world return home. New to me.

Do not recall climbing stairs, my short legs
needing to stretch on high risers.

Was I was carried one floor up? Muffled voices
settle like hens behind another door

opened to the musk of old women seated
around a room rustling with energy.

Pulled onto a lap, kissed, cuddled and passed
like a ball, no, like a Christmas gift,

I am shifted one Polish granny to another.
Land in the last lap, wet-cheeked, enveloped

in soft arms, the room explodes with clapping
as I cry out, "Grandma?"

(2024)

Somewhere between waking and sleep,
between this world and the next, I watch a boy

of four or five nestle in an old woman's arms.
She rocks, singing a lullaby of Galilee.

Something about a crying bird.
Do they know I stand beside them?

Beyond us, how far I cannot say, a line of women
shimmers in half-light. Each holds a child.

The boy beside me fidgets, dark eyes darting.
Furtive, he buries his face in the woman's bosom.

Does he know he has died?
A younger woman, in pantsuit and hijab,

walks a beam of light toward him. Leans over,
whispers. And the old one croons,

"Hardship never lasts forever, never lasts—"
Hand in hand, the younger one leads him

from the hall of grandmothers. Radiant,
neither of them looks back.

Book of the Dead

The first was down the street.
My older friend and I inspected his garage,
Nancy Drew wannabes.

She said he rigged his tailpipe,
closed the garage door. I felt an awe,
distant, yet near as the odor of exhaust.

Then my bestie's dad, who called me Monkey,
gave piggyback rides, left his Ford Fairlane
running, jumped off the George Washington Bridge.

Next year, a school assignment: "Notice something
on your way home that was not there this morning.
Use details." "I saw cops zip a black body bag

over a man in his driveway. From across the street,
I could see his blue face, so I knew what he'd done."
Teacher did not appreciate my details.

When Old Mona's son left her basement apartment
for the last time on a stretcher, I watched
the EMT cover Willie's face and

didn't cry until Willie's curls bounced
when the wheels hit cracks in the sidewalk
as if he were nodding.

The daughter of a family friend went out
the window of a San Francisco Victorian. Tripping
on acid, she thought she could fly.

Her sister showed me the clipping, convinced
me a bogeyman under my bed would grab my ankle.
So, I'd leap to safety each night.

I wondered if these deaths steeled me for
your desperate end. They didn't.
The bogeyman just moved into the closet.

Bird Fish

Op Art print, M.C. Escher, 1938

Last night's moon danced in the dark.
Lifted, a bubble in the southern sky

also called the Celestial Sea. And
you were here beside me, Brother,

beaming your goofy smile. Mock-
squeezing the moon's pearled face

between thumb and forefinger until
the man cried, Oh! We'd divvy up

constellations like marbles. Mine:
the whale, yours: the winding river

of stars Phaethon fell into
crashing the chariot of the sun.

Time stretches, snaps like saltwater
taffy. Planets scatter like aggies.

Like you, gone so far, so long
I cannot puzzle you together again.

The Great Blue's throaty rasp sounds
like your saxophone reed squealing.

Twilight's dinosaur swims in the sky.
Seconds between wingbeats are centuries

repeated in Escher's tessellations—
fish become birds, become fish.

The Double Nest

...emotion recollected in tranquility...
—William Wordsworth

First the honking, then the goose airborne
under a day moon over Dark Brook.

I find twin nests connected, bolstered by a light
fixture suspended near the basement door.

Each a robin's weave of grasses. Mud-set
cups emptied of their famous blue cargo.

...the unseen birds singing in the mist...

a line from Dorothy's Grasmere journal.
Her prose can be vital as her brother's verse.

Reunited after being separated as orphans,
they lived together until he passed.

In one nest, a hole. Cracked shell at my feet.
The risk living is. Sudden death. Your fall,

Steve. I ripped the shower curtain in two
at the news. Memories loop a mobius strip.

... the moon shone like herrings in the water...

Ours was a beatbox kind of groove.
I worked the lyrics while you laid down a beat.

Nests placed on the mantle, I touch the egg-shaped
gap in one. Place the hollow shell in the nest bowl.

Visitation

My eye catches his eye and dagger bill
jutting from behind my neighbor's azalea bush—
a juvenile heron landed across the street,
not at the creek back of our place.

Bird and I both bemused,
he stretches legs, tentative divining rods
under a shag of gray-brown feathers.
He will come toward me.
I feel it in my waters.

      Watching from my window, I lay down
my book. Curious, the heron crosses the street
into our yard, heads to the front door, struggles
at the stoop's first step as I often do.

I move behind the plate glass and he retreats,
flapping. Looks back at me from the next lawn.
Webbed toes spread as if sensing a ley line,
he dances in a circle before taking off.

How else does one mired in mud
stand without sinking or walk
so delicately on the Earth?

Rhythm Changes

Cormorant spreads wings like a priest's arms
at the top of the dam. And something in me turns—
chuntering at the memory of my brother's funeral
held years ago, without me.

Again, I envision mourners process nave to narthex.
Horns blare tribute from the choir loft. Gulls squawk
interrupting my reverie, recall Steve's improv
as bebop birds dive for pieces of bagel.

Steve wailed toward joy like Charlie Parker, his idol.
As a boy, he stepped into the aisle to see wine
become blood. Called out, echoing sanctus bells.
Early in the '60s, anything was still possible.

    Mom yanked him back into the pew
but his would be a jazz altar. His acolyte, I was
awed at "I Got Rhythm" converted into Parker's tune
"Chasin' the Bird" floated over the same chords.

Before I moved away, before Steve's breakdown
and living out of his Datsun, before I understood how
ill he was, if I ever did, before someone broke into
his car, stole his sax,

he played the Kennedy Center, toured Europe,
dreamed of composing a new sacred music—
motets and cantatas featuring reed instruments
instead of human voices.

    Our final time together, midnight
at the last mass for both of us. Just we two,
chuckling like gulls, receiving, recollecting.
Water through sluice gates approaches melody.

Invasives

Under the cacophony of birds
whose calls I cannot decipher

I sit, beside the morning glories feeling
weathered as the lattice they climb.

Some trumpet heavenly blues. Others,
twirled tight as closed umbrellas.

A crimped blossom leans on trellis.
Her moment passed, I sigh and look away.

Mull over the anatomy of a flower,
a melancholy.   Turned back,

the dented bloom now fully open.
A reverse memento mori—

Remember: you, too, must die—
but not yet.   A mockingbird solos

its profusion of confusion,
the dahlias   shredded by some bug.

Beginnings, endings are tangled vines.
Monarchs absent the milkweed, moss

still grows between patio bricks. And the
dawn redwood thought dead, half-buried

in the woods, now rises green above
poison sumac reaching for light.

Lughnasadh / Lammas

Harvest holidays on August 1st

The brook flows between two reservoirs.
I would also stream, seek my level.
Follow the weather of my days—
moments in this dell's microclimate.

I weave a chain of grief and gladness,
gather daisies like unborn children. Apologies!
as hose in hand, I stumble through
the orb spider's web.

Twin selves, pagan and churched,
rest into summer greens, here, where a
trowel is dug into a planter of bolted arugula.
And the ruby-throated feed at jewelweed.

Alone, not lonesome, the lackadaisical gardener
and the mourning dove's mellow coo,
afternoon's bass note.

Learning One Good Place

A clean breeze blows hard all day.
Listen as the wind gusts—east wind, soul wind.
Hawk crees, turkey chortles in the greenwood.
Each creature crying, "This is what I came here for."

I listen as the wind gusts—east wind, soul wind.
Watch the bee, blown past the rosa rugosa, correct course.
Each creature crying, "This is what I came here for."
Bumbling, we pollen-wallow in the blown rose.

Dusk

Ode to My Belly

Bell-shaped, you sound
growling with hunger.
Round me out from sternum

down to the space between hip bones.
Hitting bottom, you rest in the bowl
formed there

hammocked by pubic bones
you lie pliable as a sow's ear purse
silken, stretching to hold a meal.

Pour out enzymatic juices
break down bits of lamb and potato
pass along the more fibrous celery

and psyllium husks. Emptied, you fold in
on yourself, spasm with hunger again.
Mounded like yeasty bread dough

you ripen, skin thinned through the years
by kneading of a husband's hands, torso,
and babies that bulged like curled ferns.

You spill abundant over jeans, perhaps
over a dancing belt. Shall I wear a navel jewel
while you undulate, rhythmic,

corded with fat and muscle in striated layers
like so many colored scarves? Then roll you
swaying in sensuous movement

bordered by one iliac crest then the other,
snapped swinging in seismic shifts
pulchritudinous while I perambulate

with accented foot tap and spinal slip
to loll and laze luxurious in fleshy splendor.
Yellah, Habibi, Yellah!

I celebrate your appetites, my piquant friend,
always present yet always changing,
my belly, my own.

Furculas

Give me the turkey carcass cracked
to fit my pot, and I'll pick skin, shred meat
stew what is close to bone.

Outside my window, a sapling bends
held under taller pine branches. Spring-loaded,
a youngster caught in the understory.

Perch spine gleams in a bed of silt
toothed clean by muskrat, pebbles, water.
Turkey wishbone fuses clavicles, shelters

heart, lungs for the rigor of flight. Flexed,
it adds spring to upstrokes of the wild bird
flying into the pine at dusk.

Sacred to Etruscans, wishbones of chickens
were talismans rubbed for good fortune.
Like the Romans, we dub winners, losers

with a lucky break. We have no need of furculas.
Do not mount the air with our bodies. Give me
the frame of an idea to flesh out, pare down,

discover a hinge. The weight of words—
a float of spider silk, blur of bird winged my mind
to yours, marvelous runes inking the page.

Celestial Bodies

These days I see my body as a planet.
Its hills and valleys as sagging dunes,

pocked craters. And hidden galaxies bulge,
slipped discs in the body of deep space.

Nothing stays the same, though many things
return. Even Saturn's rings are seasonal.

And false dawn is sunlight reflected off
dust circling the sun. Sun that shines

like the flashlight you once held under
your bedsheet to read late into the night.

"My battery is low, and it's getting dark,"
Opportunity's last message. Mars Rover,

Red Rover, come over in radio waves like
the ones hippos sound roaring underwater.

Their partially submerged heads surface,
eyes bulging, tiny ears wriggling.

Even Pluto has a heart splattered on it.
Result of a cold slow-moving collision.

And a Hebrew sage is reported to have said,
stars are sentinels, always watching.

The Mending

> *School children of America!*
> *Help save your fathers, brothers, neighbors*
> *by collecting milkweed pods.*
>   —from a Soil Conservation Service pamphlet, 1945

The last clematis pours over the fence, so much
spilled cream. Seeds burst milkweed pods.

A chrysalis hangs its tiny lantern.
Three gilt dots seal wings within

like rivets or molten metal that heals
cracked pottery. Milkweed tufts loft into air,

land seed parachutes. Call to mind the brochure
Dad saved when the plant covered the prairie.

Millions of pounds of fluff salvaged for
the war effort. Two pillow cases full stuffed

one life vest. Hollow spindles trapped air,
the waxy coating shed water, saved a pilot

or a sailor from drowning. Emergent imagoes—
imaginal cells, dry your wings.

Flap and glide heedless of the names
we call you: Monarch, Common Wanderer.

Ride the wind to a home seen from above
this tangle of green and gold.

Remembering the Frog State

The dream of the frog sounds best at a distance—most dreamy.
        —Thoreau's journal, May 3, 1852

How to say what happened then, as a car passenger
at 60 mph just this: the land spoke to me.
No, I entered Earth like a mole tunneling under
grassy swells or like peepers in a marsh.
Consciousness having taken residence in the ground.

Boundaries dripped like Dali's clock over some edge.
Familiar sense of self slipped. Cracked as the face
of an aging burgher in a Flemish painting.
Dead wood jutted from the bog beckoning as if
I were close to it, which I was not.

As if in a canoe of an afternoon, sun glimmering
on water, I lifted out, wrapped rope around waist,
boat secured to body and barefoot touched bottom.
Only, I was not in a canoe nor in the swamp
but in a Honda on the highway.

Still, legs felt heavy in water reaching down
into the muck filled with bog orchids, lilies.
Dug in, toes in silt spread webbed, following
stems welling up toward lilypads on the surface
where glazed skin is warmed by the sun.

The Flying Monk—1055 A.D.

A descent of woodpeckers,
a building of rooks, a flight of swallows—
names for flocks listed in *The Book of St. Albans*.

What must the clattering of jackdaws
      circling the abbey made of this singular
young Benedictine, Eilmer of Malmesbury.

Fitted with leather bindings on his wrists and ankles,
rigged cruciform to sail-like wings,
a novice dreaming of Icarus.

      Jumping off the priory tower,
he'd become a kite riding air currents rising
off the hills above the river Avon.

Heart falcon-fast, he'd glide a couple of furlongs
in a rush of release. Gawking townsfolk below
spotting him as far as Oliver's Lane before

stopped in frictive air—in the pitch and roll,
he seemed to back up like the retrograde planets
plotted on his astrology charts.

Was the fall dreamlike before terror set in?
Did he wish for water instead of packed earth?
      Both legs broken

and grounded by his abbott to stop him trying again,
the lame monk studied skeins of geese,
galaxies of grackles, the motions of heavenly bodies.

Eilmer concluded his failure to soar
      was due to lack of what any bird needed—
a tail for stability, lift.

He might agree we learned to speak, to sing
having mimicked birdsong.
And by watching birds fly, we take to the sky

among a dissimulation of birds,
an abomination of monks, a worship of writers,
just another critter in the forest.

Contacting My Muse

Muse: Do you keep an altar?

Poet: Yes, of course.

Muse: What to do you place on it?

Poet: A twist of cedar driftwood, sequoia cone, an aloe and a rosemary plant.

Muse: Why these?

Poet: To remind me where I have been. To celebrate their thingness, my own.

Muse: And the bird feeder on the windowsill?

Poet: I can only hold my hand out for so long. Now I have questions for you.

Muse: I thought you might.

Poet: On the nature of things.

Muse: You mean names?

Poet: I suppose so.

Muse: Most will tell you if you ask.

Poet: But some are shy. Does each thing have more than one? Say that cardinal. What are some of his?

Muse: Tree flame. Water Pipe. Armonica.

Poet: And that breeze through the pines, West wind?

Muse: Yes, also Armonica.

Poet: And that trio of tall pines. Three Sisters?
What are some of yours?

Muse: Bridge. Hidden Treasure. And...

Poet: I can guess. Armonica.

Jerome's Lion

> *Good, better, best, never let it rest until*
> *your good is better and your better is best.*
> —attributed to Jerome of Stridon, 370–420 A.D.

Not a fan of his theology, I do like the engraving
of the monk writing, a terrier and lion dozing on
his study floor. The print on my wall, a peaceful scene

unlike the torturous hours just spent watching
the tragicomedy: "Who's Afraid of Virginia Woolf?"
A penance, for what I'm not sure.

In the film's party from hell, Professor George taunts
his guests, quipping, "Good, better, bested!"
I marvel at his wife Martha's sustained rage.

Gut tightening at rounds of putdowns,
I rewind mind-movies of my parents' fights,
of my own snarky attitude, my bark.

Seek some luminous stopgap, a limbo or bardo
where Beyonce and Beelzebub coexist.
A science of self that aims for parity. Softens

"Bastard!" and "Bitch!" to the milder tones
the couple speak in by the film's, by illusion's end.
Like sighs the saint might release, fingers aching

with cramp, after chiding the lion to retract claws
into his padded paw slung over the whimpering dog,
both beasts asleep and dreaming.

Coming to Terms

A pair of crows swoop down on a young rabbit.
Wings explode, furred hind legs kick high.
I throw a stone to disrupt the hunt, for now.

Local crows also dive-bomb my husband.
They do not like his baseball cap.
Remember faces. Are not fans of masks.

What would they make of a plague doctor's
leather top hat, black robes and beaked mask
filled with herbs against miasmas? Would they

recognize it as Corvid-like or might it merely
appear monstrous? More than a character in
Commedia dell'arte, plague doctors donned early
PPE, let blood, witnessed wills, counted dead bodies.

At dusk, we drive by crows pecking at roadkill—
a cottontail chased onto asphalt. I sigh. Breathing in,
imagine the savory scent of rosemary and juniper.
My husband tugs at his cap. We drive on.

The Rental

At the vacation cottage by the sea,
the doe with her fawns in the thicket,

and we who roll bocce balls through the
afternoon while the lawn is dry, sun overhead.

Firewood goes damp with drizzle, and we are
bordered by sleep as the lot is edged with thistle.

Waves echo the swish of a recent cardiogram—
murmuring muscle, hollow but for the pulsing.

The gift listed for this anniversary is land.
And this stone crop rises from the sea like the

carapace of a leatherback, largest turtle.
Or a discrete thought from out the mist.

Island mind comes on after island time
seeps up, groundwater surfacing. Sans screens,

I see a bird's shadow cast on the grass. Notice
cicadas wind to crescendo. Monarchs flutter

and feed before wending south. We two
are paused like the butterflies gathering fuel.

Enthroned in rattan, we smile for pictures
our adult kids snap. Fingers entwined, we

join what has been with whatever is to come.
Above us a mating pair, bodies clasped,

wings through salt air. No wonder we love
stories for their beginnings, middles, and ends

paralleling our lives and those of leatherbacks
who, since the reign of the dinosaurs

have laid egg clutches in sandy shore nests
chambered like the heart.

Wisdom Is a Bird

Z333, tag on the world's oldest known bird.
Not petrel nor shearwater, but a Laysan albatross.
From the Book of Wisdom—*she is bright and does
not grow dim.* Now over seventy and a mother again.

Her chicks wait for a meal, gobble bits of plastic
waste washed ashore. The survivors fledged,
she glides on the longest wings, soars for hours,
days without flapping.

*She deploys her strength from one end of the earth
to the other.* Can circle the globe in two months.
Vulnerable floating in waves, she may sleep mid-air.
Skim over oceans following fishing trawlers

...active...sharp...unperturbed...all-surveying.

Returned each year to Hawaii's far archipelago,
face to face with her lifelong mate, heads bob and
shake in their mirrored dance. Hooked bills
clatter, feign preening, each dancer's head tucked

briefly under a wing. Neck craned, he echoes her
crooning moan. Webbed feet stomp the beat
to excited whistles again, again. And like him,
I fall in love with her beauty.

Dark Brook

You must come down,
down to the level of wild flowing.
You can hear it while indoors
but seated brookside,
water is all you hear. Fiddle-fast,
yet soothing as a strummed harp
it drowns out cars, neighbors
and the hum of distant trains.
Leaves skitter as day unwinds.
Silk lines of jumping spiders
shiver as you feel yourself merge
with all you see—mind mirroring
low breezes ranging over the dell,
over your body, clicking into place
remembrance of other seasons.
This afternoon in the darkening year,
offers more than a need for closure,
for dominion. Enough to be
by freshwater rushing white over
rock and leaf, sleek in the flow.
Late sun on late skin, the moment fluent
as the brook departing soon as it arrives.

Nest Fidelity in Two Movements

All afternoon I watch this wren tag team
feed loud chicks with flies and beetles.
The offices of instinct, of love, just keep serving.

And a brown cowbird harasses a sparrow.
Demands every other worm the smaller bird pries
from the ground. I know people like this.

Called a brood parasite, cowbirds lay eggs
in other bird's nests. Rely on them to incubate,
even feed their offspring.

Some birds care for the cowbird chicks,
others build nests on top of the interloper's egg
or beside it rather than take on more. Nearby,

a cardinal stands in the birdbath. One green
leg hangs from his beak, orange as a traffic cone.
The praying mantis become prey.

Maybe surrender is the whole-making twin
of despair. Not identical but fraternal, sororal.
An acceptance of what is.

***

The double nest gone now from the undercroft,
robin has returned to her nesting site.
Claimed the vacant phoebe's nest a few feet

from her old one. Weaving grass,
she enlarged the cup from the edges out
by twining rootlets with the wrist of her wing.

After a soaking rain, nest to earth, over and over,
she packed it with mud from her beak
to bond the snug, hold it together.

Balanced in the wisteria that climbs the croft,
the refashioned nest cradles three new lives
reeled, as I am, into the beautiful Real.

Homing

Song sparrow close as skin
does not sing but chirps little blasts
like the breeze wafting my cheek.

My upper lip twitches with what's coming.
Something juicy as belladonna berries
vining between porch boards.

Shall I cut them back? No.
I crave the comfort of creeping things
overcoming structure like stone ruins

cloaked in ivy. Or fog fingering
the brook in this overcast,
lowering expectations.

Fine weather is overrated. I want to settle.
Sit as stones sit. Take breath into lungs
flung across my diaphragm—

saddlebags on the pack mule of my body.
Air breathed out, then returned like the bird
to this roost of bone and flesh.

Dark

Desire Path

Clutch of eggs, nest of rabbits, knot of toads,
all found at the road's end where the brook bends.

Between our house and the house flanked by woods
a corridor runs, highway for the least seen.

Snapping turtle walks there, tire tracks grooved
into her cracked shell. Call her survivor

returned to lay eggs in mulch. The neighbor boy
names her Grampy. No guile in him, nor in the

gravid turtle waiting to secret her eggs. No fear
in the local cooper's hawk all flap and splash,

a stone's throw from me on the shore. Mink
clamber to their burrow dug under the garage.

A stilled weathervane, heron scouts bullfrogs
and bluegills from the shed roof. Once,

I watched a bobcat in the woods eye the boy
chasing his sister along the grass beaten trail.

Same trail coyotes patrol after midnight,
cutting through these suburban haunts.

Grounded

for Greta Thunberg

Remember riding your bike and never
wanting to go in even for supper?

And dancing, not the paired off kind,
we are going to the time of freedom.

Time of wild body thrusts and leaps
before you cared who was watching.

Raise your hand if you recall the feel
of grass beneath bare feet and

not caring if an ant crawled along
your arm lifting hairs there

one by one, even liking it.
Remember hearing water ring

before being told otherwise?
Don't sing a sad tune, though you are

swimming with the crocodiles now.
Count your fingers, count your toes

while you still can. We're talking about
the righteous anger of youth.

Dogged persistence, serious sadness
of Buster Keaton born of resistance to

"the way things are." Praises be to Greta
for her wry smile, even as it's getting dark.

One Day, May 25, 2020

A raven is not a crow, a magpie not a jay,
and the Black man holding a metal object in the park
is birdwatching with binoculars.

A gathering of ravens is called a conspiracy,
an unkindness. Yet, one will offer consolation to
another who's been mobbed.

And crows hold funerals for their dead.
We homo sapiens have only two inborn fears,
fear of falling and fear of loud sounds.

Our phobias are legion. Ornithophobia is fear
of our feathered friends. After the premiere of *The Birds*,
gull screeches blasted from theater loudspeakers.

During filming, Hitchcock had live ravens and gulls
hurled at a shocked Tippi Hedren who writhed on the floor,
take after take. In the trailer, Hitch spoke of:

*caging, stuffing, plucking feathers for hats, slaughtering
birds for meat*. Then with faux sincerity, he asked
why they should hate us.

My rescued cat recoiled at the sight of our sofa.
Eventually, head lowered stalking, he braved it tapping
the couch with paw, checking for signs of life.

Dread of being arrested, even for no reason is capiophobia.
Fear of going to jail carcerophobia. And one who
considers all humans members of a single community

is a cosmopolite. May one day, buying cigs
at the corner store, birding or simply curbing your dog
be a walk in the park.

Darwin's Tree and Escher's Birds

Lines branch off his notebook sketch—
generations of giraffes, humans represented
in Darwin's Tree of Life, Tree of Time.

Metaphor of the many sprung
from one point, say a clock's center,
where hour and minute hands are pinned.

The biologist's figure reminds me
of a clock I defaced. Frustrated while
calling my family repeatedly for supper,

I twisted the clock's wire hands
with my hands. Left them bent, protruding
at odd angles. So satisfying.

My pop art statement that only the bold
or curious ever enquire after.
Some of Darwin's lines are ended

segments representing excising events—
a sea cow or mayfly no longer extant.
And Escher fashioned my favorite

timepiece of wood inlay for the
Leiden town hall. Backgrounded
in blond elm, dozens of mahogany birds

circle, carved in the clockface.
They peel off flying in ordinal directions,
a chime of wrens winging.

The Problem

At first it's algebra, x + y =
initials carved in a tree. Memorization
of formulas with many possible substitutions.

More settle it's three-dimensional,
geometric, more memorization of formulas,
the circle's radius from center to edge.

In the end, despite what people say,
it comes down to logic. Three small dots
form its crucible with so much space between.

If, then, therefore—
the triad in answer to the question:
Do you love me?

Soldiers, gang members ask it of each other.
Answer, "If you do, then you'll wait for me,
kill or die for me, remember me, remember."

The teenager leaving home asks it of parents
willing to die for her. Just as hard to remember
the hurled barbs and await her return.

The stroke victim can speak just three words
(stand-ins for everything). He repeats them
to his wife who passes him pencil and paper,

waits for the cribbed script, legible stitches
teased from the hem of language, translation of,
"What to do... what to do... what to do?"

The Symbiocene: wished-for time of deeper integration between humans and all the natural world

In the words of Don La Fontaine, voice-over king
of movie trailers and commercials for Mega Millions,

"We have to very rapidly establish the world we are
transporting them to." In a world where

Ted Bundy is a TV interview celeb, another choice:
Extraordinary Birder with Christian Cooper.

In our world, a banditry of titmice, nuthatches form
a foraging guild while on TCM, outlaw Mae West,

six-shooters in hand, dispatches movie warriors.
Bullets rain down in a celluloid shower of feathers.

And a randy W.C. Fields croaks, "My little chickadee!"
Actors have traded places with the audience,

more guns than people now. In a world where
solastalgia replaces nostalgia, may shoreline cede to

marsh, parklands cared for by native peoples who
keep them in balance. May Mr. La Fontaine,

Thunder Throat, the Voice of God, have narrated the
Anthropocene's end with trailers for: *Dr. Strangelove,*

The Elephant Man, Terminator 2. Enter Yo-Yo Ma
seated in a forest glade, cello whistling like wind

as he accompanies a host of sparrows, a fall of warblers
singing us all into the coming age.

Blues for Betty

> *...the engine passed by at six o'clock*
> *and the cab passed by at nine.*
> —lyrics to the song "In the Pines"

Neighbor Betty nursed her husband in their post-war Cape.
Lost him to cancer. Shook her head at the work of it.

The year before, their paroled son (no one would hire),
shot himself in the back bedroom after supper.

I thought that loud crack was a downed tree.
Maybe the pines hear thoughts we don't dare speak.

Standing clustered, take in what we breathe out,
store it in bark as chemical memory.

Brushed boughs do wail in wind. And the soul travels—
a small breeze or bird brooding in tangled moss.

In the pines, in the pines, where the sun never shines

Betty seldom left her place except to buy groceries
or play the fifty cent slots. She told me she had no talent.

Yet, her wry quips delivered with timing like George Burns,
amused fellow day-trippers on the bus ride to the casino.

Bedside at Betty's leave-taking, her chest heaved, rattling
like steel rail joints. I listened as quiet as wood.

No visitors for a week and the night nurse nodding,
I held her hand, whispered she could cut loose.

My girl, my girl, where will you go?

Come spring, a young couple moved into the place.
Hawks nested in the tallest pine. I called them Jack and Betty.

Their aerie swayed in the evergreen, twigs and feathers drifting.
Strange nests: these bodies, this Earth.

Cat and Mouse

Anytime, anywhere, always ready, always there.
—Navy submarine motto

The going hell for leather words printed under
a smiling skull on the back of the man's bomber jacket
standing in front of me in the grocery line.

And what does happen at the moment of death?
Do we faint into another consciousness as in
poet Liz Bishops's waiting room? Will it hurt?

When our Siamese left us "gifts" of dead prey
Mom said, "Nature stuns the mouse with a chemical
blunting the horror, the pain."

Coping mechanisms can become malignant,
cells in overdrive morph into cancer. The amaryllis
stem cracks under the weight of a triple blossom.

My dead are easier to love now. Pet peeves
I held against them clarify like melted butter.
Their essences now faint perfumes.

Will I hear my rendezvous approach
like the tick tock of Captain Hook's croc,
or will it arrive torpedo deep, silent, fast?

May death be a cat that claims my lap,
animal heart beating against thigh
as I let go a last sigh.

Bond of Union, lithograph, M.C. Escher

Young lovers as new constellation—
faces of the artist's son and daughter-in-law loom in night.

    Eyes cast downward, heads tilted toward

each other, their features spiral like orange peels
looped together. Black space seen through the gaps.

    Escher set little spheres floating
before their eyes, through throats, and up into craniums
joined at the hairlines.   Planets of possibility,

blank thought bubbles rise before the words,
    sweet and harsh, come. And they will come
surely as bills, blissful nights, disillusioned Saturdays.

    Together, their ribboned faces suggest
a ribcage guarding what needs protection. Their eyes
focus on a few spheres balanced on the edge of connection.

    Their pose recalls a photo—close-up
of our daughter and son-in-law and the sudden snowflakes
that fell the morning of their May wedding.

    Later in the warming day,
tender-tough rose petals lay strewn across the asphalt,
pale as stars.

Signs and Wonders

June 1178, five Canterbury monks watched the moon
catch fire, "writhe and throb like a wounded snake."

July 2023, milky sky and skunk stink fills our backyard.
Will moonlight overpower meteors? Not expecting

the drama stunned monks saw and scientists call a comet
or exploded meteor, under clearing skies

we may render the awe due the Perseid shower.
A screech owl repeats his descending scale.

To have been a bird at that priory window,
heard tonsured brothers talk of war, apocalypse.

Try to frame the terror come soon after Beckett lost the
crown of his head. Blood on cathedral floors.

Something wiggles at my feet. A shrew from between
stones like the trilobite encased in shale that sits

on my desk. Back arched and molting,
that ancient creature crawled out of her skull, split open.

Bits of exoskeleton floated in the Cambrian Sea
as rock and ice now trail in the dark above our heads.

Slow Work

Quaking Aspen, Populus Tremuloides.
One, yet many, sprung from a single seed

like the eighty-thousand-year-old forest sprawling
across a Utah plateau, the Trembling Giant.

Briefly emptied of fixed notions—who I am,
you are, as cracked eggs spill yokes and

stargazer lilies pollen; change (a word that
can mean trouble) comes to us as storms

do to fields. If forgiveness is a flower, then
mercy is the field it grows in.

With tears to see through and spit to name
our pain (we are, after all, mostly water) and

harrowed as thatched soil. Suppled, we may
welcome others, even our various selves.

Pieced Out

after a handmade quilt

Flush with trees and a trio of ducks,
this cotton lawn sown with earth dreams
soothes tired eyes.

A meadow where daylight wends
into blue-black night
edging the cloth

and centered sun sustains.
Each square holds its circle—
an eye staring back.

A cookie unbroken.
Patchwork book of days,
I pull the spread up and over me.

Laid out on the bed, it satisfies
the hungering after beauty
ordered like piano keys. Or lights

in a windowpane, a gameboard,
clock hands or coffee with cream.
The quiet consolation of things.

Orison for the Wee Hours

Drifting into night's small death,
listening to the brook go on

after a playback of day's bedlam,
I conjure the repose of rocks

nestled into welcoming ground.
Imagine becoming rooted

as oaks whose crowns cosset
a charm of goldfinches.

Cull the bravery of chickadee,
clarity of wren's song, and

the comedic chops of titmice
to enter where dreams may come.

Before orphaned anxieties
paw at my back, I invite my dead

to shelter awhile, travel with me,
having distanced them so.

And as moonlight touches the crow's
feet cornering my husband's eyes

that seem closer to me than
my own nose, smiling, sleep.

Notes

Page 7: The italicized lines in the epigraph are from "Al Aaraaf" in *The Works of Edgar Allan Poe in Five Volumes: The Raven Edition* (P.F. Collier, 1902)

Page 11: The italicized lines are from the poem, "The Mantle of Saint Brigid" which appears with varying titles, author unknown.

Page 20: In 2015, Finnish photographer Lassi Rautiainen followed and photographed a gray wolf and brown bear who accompanied each other for ten days. He regularly photographs bears and found this to be a most unusual encounter. The photos are widely available online.

Page 21: Researchers in Australia in 2013 transplanted DNA material from frozen samples of the extinct Gastric Brooding Frog into a similar species. Though the resulting embryos lived for only a few days, the experiment was considered successful.

Page 25: The italicized line in the poem, "Almost Paradise" is from the song "Galilean Lullaby." written by the Anglo-Palestinian singer Reem Kelani.

Page 30: The phrase "...emotion recollected in tranquility" is taken from William Wordsworth's preface to the second edition of *Lyrical Ballads, Volume 1*, London, (T.N. Longman and O. Rees, 1800). "Poetry is the spontaneous overflow of powerful feelings: it takes its origin from emotion recollected in tranquility." And the italicized lines in my poem "The Double Nest" are excerpted from the book *Journals of Dorothy Wordsworth* (Oxford University Press, 1971).

Page 48: Italicized lines in the poem "Wisdom Is a Bird" are from the *Book of Wisdom*, Jerusalem Bible (Galilee Books, 1971).

Page 54: The poem "One Day May 25, 2020" refers to the incident in Central Park when Black birdwatcher Christian Cooper had a false police report made against him. He was later featured in a Disney Channel show on birding. That same day George Floyd was murdered by a policeman Derek Chauvin in Minneapolis.

Page 57: The Symbiocene is a term coined by Glenn Albrecht, professor and environmentalist. Solastalgia is also his term which names the distress felt by environmental change. Terms from *Earth Emotions: New Words for a New World*, (Cornell University Press, 2019).

Title Index

After the Gold Rush 40
Almost Paradise 44
Approaching Equinox 24
Ask the Animals 32
At Slack Tide 33
Available Music 28
Bear and Wolf 37
Beast with No Name 42
Bird Fish 48
Bird Hours 14
Blues for Betty 82
Bond of Union, lithograph, M.C. Escher 85
Bonfire (2021) 25
Book of the Dead 46
Brookside 36
Cat and Mouse 84
Celestial Bodies 59
Cold Snap 20

Coming to Terms	67
Contacting My Muse	64
Dark Brook	71
Darwin's Tree and Escher's Birds	79
Desire Path	76
Entranced	31
Floating Arms	26
Forced Spring	27
Furculas	58
Grounded	77
Homing	74
House Holds	18
Invasives	52
Jerome's Lion	66
Lament	43
Learning One Good Place	54
Lughnasadh / Lammas	53
Nest Fidelity in Two Movements	72
Ode to My Belly	56
On De-extinction	38
One Day, May 25, 2020	78
Orison for the Wee Hours	89
Pedal Pushers	22
Pieced Out	88
Poemania	21
Remembering the Frog State	61
Rhythm Changes	51
Rose-breasted Grosbeak	29
Shadows	19
Signs and Wonders	86
Slow Work	87
Sub-Versive	17
The Doorway Effect	16
The Double Nest	49

The Flying Monk—1055 A.D. 62
The Little Hours 30
The Mending 60
The Problem 80
The Rental 68
The Symbiocene: wished-for time of deeper integration
    between humans and all the natural world 81
Visitation 50
When Wood Dies 39
Wisdom Is a Bird 70

First Line Index

A
A clean breeze blows hard all day 54
A descent of woodpeckers 62
A gang of street urchins 17
All afternoon I watch this wren tag team 72
A pair of crows swoop down on a young rabbit 67
A raven is not a crow, a magpie not a jay 78
At first it's algebra, x + y = ... 80
At the vacation cottage by the sea 68

B
Before I sight him, the shy bird 29
Before the storm, before I shoot 20
Bell-shaped, you sound 56
Bulb of the buried flower 27

C
Clutch of eggs, nest of rabbits, knot of toads 76
Cormorant spreads wings like a priest's arms 51

D
Do you keep an altar? 64
Draped in sheers, my cat contemplates 31
Drifting into night's small death 89

E
Eyes open to the uncommon 16

F
First the honking, then the goose airborne 49
Flush with trees and a trio of ducks 88
From what direction does it come? 28

G
Give me the turkey carcass cracked 58

H
He shakes off den dreams, splashes 37
Housewarming to mortgage burning 18
How to say what happened then, as a car passenger 61

I
I call to myself today the musicality 36
Icy branches glisten 24
In the words of Don La Fontaine, voice-over king 81
I reach for Dad's hand as he rings the bell 44
I would enter like a cow wandering in and out 43

J
June 1178, five Canterbury monks watched the moon ...86

L
Last night's moon danced in the dark 48
Like a murmuration of starlings 42
Lines branch off his notebook sketch 79

M
Mid-morn, noon, mid-afternoon 30
Moonbeam, moon dream. Man-in-the-moon 40
My eye catches his eye and dagger bill 50

N
Neighbor Betty nursed her husband in their post-war Cape 82
Not a fan of his theology, I do like the engraving 66
Now that I no longer take long walks 33

Q
Quaking Aspen, Populus Tremuloides 87

R
Remember riding your bike and never 77
Ribbon of first light 14

S
She's rock-sitting in my mind's eye 38
Snow in patches 25
Sometimes memories pile in a wreck of years 21
Song sparrow close as skin 74

T
The bike hangs on our shed wall 22
The brook flows between two reservoirs 53
The eve before the Irish first day of spring 26
The first was down the street 46
The going hell for leather words printed under 84
The last clematis pours over the fence, so much 60
These days I see my body as a planet 59
They also occupy rooms 19

U
Under a cacophony of birdsong 52

W
Windblown swamp maple 39
Wolf spider on a flat rock splays 32

Y
You must come down 71
Young lovers as new constellation 85

Z
Z333, tag on the world's oldest known bird 70